# waterfront|HOMES

# waterfront|HOMES

**Author:** Paco Asensio

**Editor:** Quim Rosell

**Translation:** Michael Bunn

**Proofreading:** Juliet King

**Design and layout:** Mireia Casanovas Soley

### Photographers:

Peter Durant/ARCBLUE (*Boat Pavilion*); Alberto Piovano (*Ugarte House, Reutter House*); Edward Niles (*S House*); Andrés Lejona (*Gontovnik House*); Philip Gumuchdjian + Sandro Michahelles (*The House of Thought*); Eugeni Pons (*House in Corfu, House at Calella de Palafrugell, Tsirigakis House*); Stellan Herner (The *Villa at Dalarö*); Anthony Browell (*Scobie House*); Fernando Alda (*González House*); Katsuhida Kida (*House in Japan*); Undine Pröhl (*Capistrano Beach House*); Fujitsuka Mitumasa (*Water Glass House*); Alberto Muciaccia (*House in Orta Lake*); Jo Reld + John Peck/Tim Brotherton (*Baggy House*); Jean-Daniel Pasquettaz (*Summer House*); Cecilia Innes (*Boathouse*); Paul Ott (*GucklHupf*)

**2000 © Loft Publications s.l. and HBI,
an imprint of HarperCollins Publishers**

Paperback ISBN: 0-8230-7408-0
Hardcover ISBN: 0-688-17978-9

Printed in Spain
Apipe Gráficas, s.l.

First published in 2000 by LOFT and HBI,
an imprint of HarperCollins Publishers
10 East 53rd St.
New York, NY 10022-5299

Distributed in the U.S. and Canada
by Watson-Guptill Publications
1515 Broadway
New York, NY 10036
Telephone: (800)-451-1741
(732)- 363-4511 in NJ, AK, HI
Fax: (732)-363-0338

Distributed throughout the rest of the world
by HarperCollins International
10 East 53rd St.
New York, NY 10022-5299

**Editorial project:**
**LOFT** publications
Domènec 9, 2-2
08012 Barcelona. Spain
Phone: +34 93 218 30 99
Fax: +34 93 237 00 60
e-mail: loft@loftpublications.com
www.loftpublications.com

"WATER IS THE EYE OF THE EARTH...
Where is reality?
In the sky or in the water's depths?..."

Victor Shklovsky

Photograph: Toni Soriano

"Waterfront" is the term we give
to those houses which have been built
on that strange, extreme point where water
meets land. The houses are constructed on the
solid and more reliable of the two elements, using
methods that respect the law of gravity. However, if
you cross the border, you find yourself in a watery world
of escapism and contemplation. In this ever-changing
physical medium, reflections are the only version of reality.
This book is a selection of works and plans in which the
designs represent an architectural response to given physical situations (distinct topography and geometry), and adopt
different strategies depending on the way the site relates to
the water nearby. Whether the houses stand by the sea, at
theedge of a lake, on the banks of a river, or overlooking a
reservoir, their proximity to the water results in unique features
and effects. What the designs share is an air of submissiveness
to the water's presence. In some cases, water and its qualities (its
reflections, color, mercurial nature, and the light it gives off) may be
considered as a passive background for the house. In other cases,
water takes on a more active role, and is directly incorporated into the
house's design as a kind of space that participates in the structure's
design and volume (for example, terraces which stretch out beyond their
confines). Water, or "liquid space," also influences the daily and nocturnal
functions of the house, the connecting routes between rooms, and other structural aspects. Proximity to water produces dramatic results in houses. For example,

the main body of the structure might extend to the point that it almost touches the water, or the house's interior space might be drawn out towards the water in the form of a platform, deck or jetty. These spaces become the threshold between the interior and the exterior. The absolute extreme is the case of "boathouses": designs that convert the house into a ship, or rather, into what appears to be a vessel that has run aground at the water's edge and transformed itself into a fixed, permanent dwelling.

Other houses are conceived as summer houses, special spaces with a minimal, yet comfortable, layout. These houses float way above the water level, like bubbles that have managed to defy the laws of gravity, enveloping the residents in watery dreams, far away from reality, and accompanied only by the distant sound of splashing water. Other residences appear to be vast structures that have just emerged from the water's depths to plant themselves on the shore. And finally, there are some houses that have been granted privileged coastal locations so high up that the views stretch as far as the eye can see: the point where water and sky are divided by the horizon.

Photograph: Alberto Piovano

United Kingdom

Brookes, Stancey, Randall

Streatley
on Thames

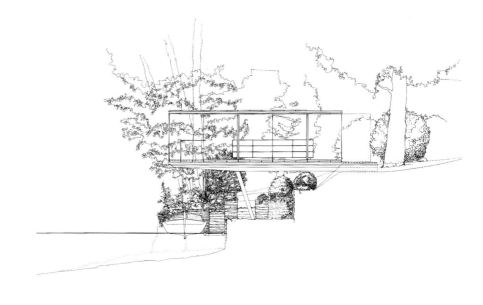

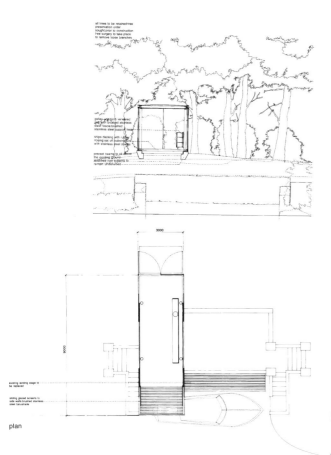

plan

## Boat Pavilion

This building's transparent encasement and relation to the water are reminiscent of a garden pavilion. In fact, the building was conceived as a space of rest adjoining the vast garden of the property on which it stands. Here, one can tranquilly contemplate the flowing waters of the River Thames.

Two other proposals were presented and turned down because they did not conform to the strict requirements of urban regulations. However, the perseverance of the client, a long-standing owner of ships, made possible the construction of a third alternative, subtly designed as if it were a jewel.

Seen from the opposite river bank, the perception of the body's volume is reduced to a minimum in order to be oriented perpendicularly to the flow of the waters. To suggest the sensation of floating, the building features an important projection over the river. Two concrete pillars, supported in the ground by a common base, connect with two beams that project out from the earth in an overhang. The body manages to extend almost all of its length without interruption beyond the edge of the river. The metallic structure and the large glass panels that form the shell of the prism achieve an effect of maximum transparency and views.

A series of the exterior spaces were carefully designed, including the platform that presides over the principal entry and the stairs that descend to the level of the river in order to reach the dock.

Two of the key features in this plan: the powerful supporting structure, which makes it possible to include such prominent eaves, and the fine lines of the parallelepiped's metal framework.

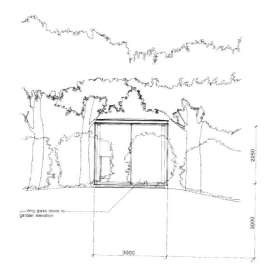

2250

3000

3000

pivoting glass doors to garden elevation

Tranverse section.

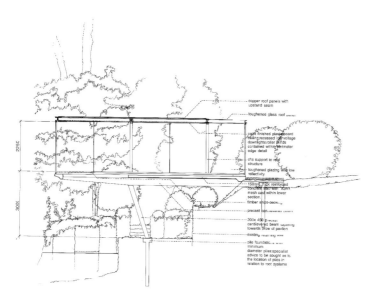

copper roof panels with upstand seam

toughened glass roof

paint finished plasterboard ceiling;recessed low voltage downlights;roller blinds contained within perimeter edge detail

chs support to roof structure

toughened glazing with low reflectivity

2250

300

150mm thick reinforced concrete slab with A393 mesh cast within lower section

timber ships deck

precast conc.

300x 450 rc cantilevered beam tapering towards brow of pavilion

existing retaining wall

pile foundation with minimum diameter piles;specialist advice to be sought as to the location of piles in relation to root systems

Longitudinal section.

elevation

river thames

Elevation: from the river.

Mathias Klotz

# Maitencillo Sur

Chile

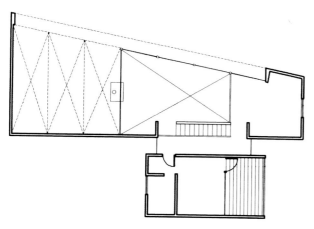

Plan of second level.

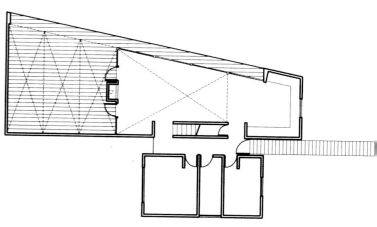

Plan of first level.

## Ugarte House

This is a weekend retreat set slightly back from the cliffs at Maitencillo Sur, 80 miles north of Santiago. The structure is reduced to the bare minimum, which enhances the effect of subtle lines and bright spaces. The design draws considerably on the traditional building methods of the region, especially in the use of exposed wood. In this construction, the wood has a rough, untreated look to it, giving the house the appearance of a mountain shelter. It is an extremely simple structure, covered by a roof that seems much too delicate for its purpose, especially when seen against the vast backdrop of the Pacific Ocean. However, when viewed from the opposite angle, looking away from the sea, the residence becomes an eye-catching construction that redefines and reinterprets the surrounding countryside.

The house is essentially made up of two sections that are separate, yet connected by a passage, which is the main point of entry and which continues into the interior. The smaller of the two sections contains the bedrooms and bathrooms, while the larger one is a two-level structure, with the kitchen, dining room and living room on the first floor, and the study on the second floor. The terraces also have an unfinished look about them, resembling gaping holes or empty spaces that have been carved out of the two sections of the house so that they are sheltered from the strong, southerly winds. The larger section has an area gouged out of it at the southern end that serves as a patio for the adjacent living room. This exterior space makes the room seem more spacious.

Ugarte house is built entirely of wood, both inside and out. The exterior has been overlaid with wooden slats, while the interior is lined with wood paneling. The exterior slats have been applied vertically on the smaller section and horizontally on the larger one, a simple touch that effectively establishes the two volumes as independent pieces. An unusual project, the house was created in part as a place in which to display the client's extensive collection of modern art.

The stairway and the fireplace:
features which are linked, yet
autonomous.

Elevation: east.

Elevation: north.

Elevation: west.

Elevation: south.

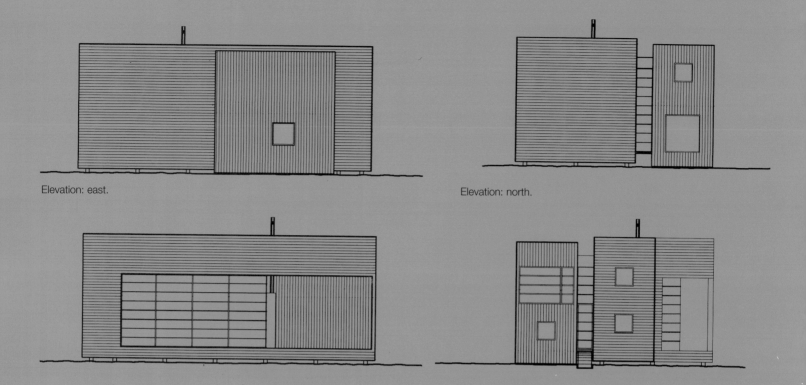

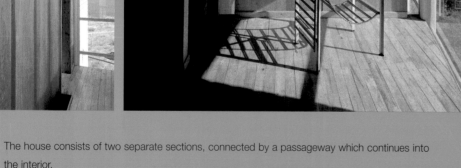

The house consists of two separate sections, connected by a passageway which continues into the interior.

The volume of the larger section represents a clear, concise geometric arrangement, in which on one side there is an empty space or a void, on the other a space which is trapped inside an all-embracing transparency, until finally reaching the wooden section.

Edward R. Niles Architect

United States

# Malibu

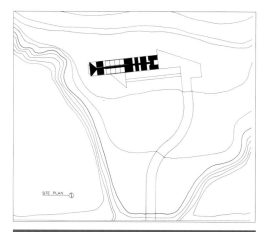

SITE PLAN

## S House

The prevailing idea behind this California house overlooking the Pacific Ocean is the play between full and empty. Of pure geometry and contrasting materials, the house is composed of various volumes that are ordered symmetrically along an axis that materializes in a unique windowed gallery that crosses the entire building.

The rhythm that produces the sequences between full and empty, transparent and opaque, culminates in the house's only bedroom: an opaque block that projects itself as an oblique form, like a funnel, over the landscape. A glazed volume hangs over this block on its widest face and opens it towards the views, connecting it to the exterior. Preceding the bedroom are two translucent, symmetrical volumes, each with a bathroom and dressing room. A large glass gallery separates them from the rest of the house, as if guarding a sacred, intimate space. When the sliding doors of the gallery are open, the space is transformed into a large open patio between the bedroom and the rest of the residence

The entire building is a succession of containers arranged along a street. One can enter the building from the patio or from the entry located on the extreme opposite of the bedroom, with two garages arranged symmetrically on both sides of the gallery. Two pairs of closed volumes containing the living and service zones precede a large, united space shared by the kitchen, dining room and salon. It is here that the interior space flows and integrates with the exterior, as if the kitchen, dining room and living room were really on the patio and the patio shared this interior space.

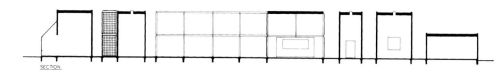

SECTION

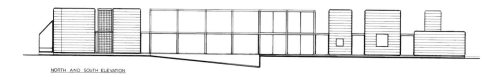

NORTH AND SOUTH ELEVATION

The geometry of this plan is very simple: right angles and cubic spaces are combined, but in a strict order: there are no curves or asymmetry allowed to creep into the design. The glazed roof of the gallery means that all of the interior spaces are well-illuminated, thereby reinforcing the three-dimensional quality of the forms inside. These are boxes, which stand separate from each other, but they are surrounded by a fluid space in which the activities of daily life go on.

As far as the spaces of the house are concerned, this is a structure with a great dramatic quality: the interior and the exterior are presented as two opposite poles which are occasionally combined to create contrasts, or separated completely, so as to accentuate their differences and exaggerate their respective qualities.

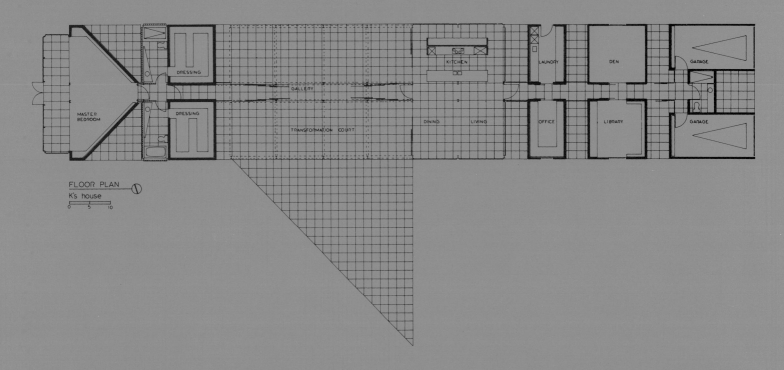

FLOOR PLAN
K's house
0    5    10

This arrangement of empty spaces and solid objects, of containers made of different materials, of rhythms and transparencies, is all laid out on a completely horizontal platform, upon which the building stands. The same floor surface runs through the interior and exterior spaces; only the closed spaces are carpeted, a feature which gives a sense of intimacy and meditation, of inwardness and privacy.

Guillermo Arias & Luís Cuartas

Pue

## Gontovnik House

In this design, volume – so simple in its appearance – was the deciding factor when it came to solving the complex problems that arose from the location and topography. Although the site is an excellent one, it does not, for the most part, offer a good view of the sea. The land, which is 16 meters wide by 55 meters long and flanked by party walls, slopes up from the street side to the top of a rocky crag. The volume, therefore, has been sliced into different levels, giving the impression of a stairway rising up to a vantage point where there is a spectacular view of the Caribbean. This first "slice" or step of the building is down at street–level and contains the garages, the guestrooms and children's bedrooms. The next section up, the middle slice, is the entrance to the house and the place where the main corridors converge. It also contains the kitchen and the dining room, all arranged around a central patio. This patio, apart from helping to keep the house cool, is a major source of light for the building. Finally, up on the crag, is the third and top slice of the house, which contains the living room and the master bedroom, both with windows that look out over the cliff. From the bedroom, there is access to the roof, which is laid out like a kind of garden–terrace, another example of how the design maximizes the useable space provided by the split–level construction.

The successful execution of an architectural plan usually depends, among other factors, on the relation between the design and the location. This design went a little further. The idea was a structure suitable both as a permanent residence and a second home by the sea.

In this case it was the architectural object itself that provided the solution not only to the problems of the site, but also to the ambivalence of the program. This is a plan that speaks for itself regarding the way in which architecture is capable of creating ideal living spaces without having to resort to sophisticated construction methods or expensive materials.

The structures which allow light into the building were carefully designed. In the living rooms there are panoramic windows protected by shutters made up of wooden slats, to filter the rays of the sun. The bathrooms, on the other hand, have small windows which both limit the incoming light and give privacy to the people inside.

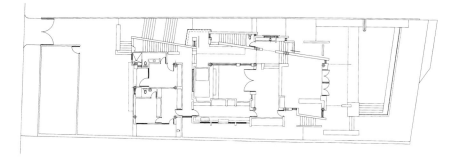

 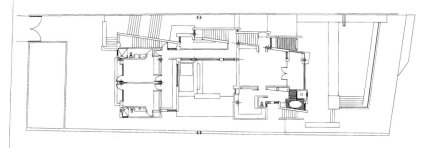

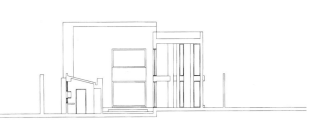 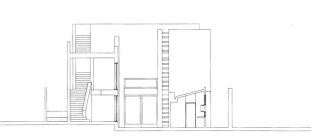

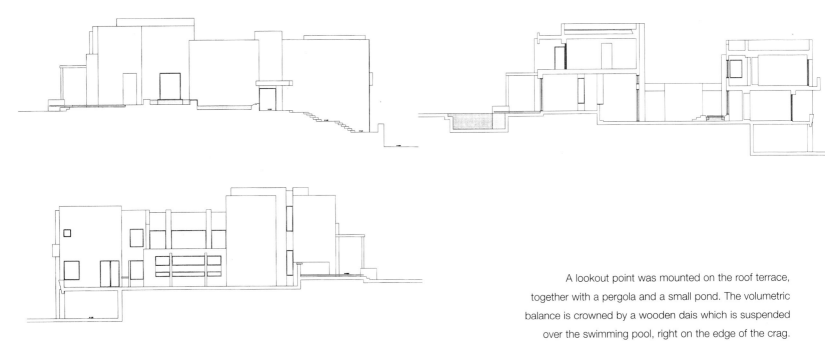

A lookout point was mounted on the roof terrace, together with a pergola and a small pond. The volumetric balance is crowned by a wooden dais which is suspended over the swimming pool, right on the edge of the crag.

# Skibbereen

Ireland

Philip Gumuchdjian

43

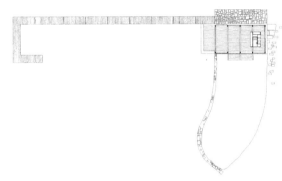

## The House of Thought

Located on the river Ilen, in the west of Ireland, this small and carefully made building was conceived as a place of meditation and retreat for the film producer Lord Puttnam of Queensgate.

The architecture reflects a wide range of references: houseboat structures, farmer's sheds, livestock stables, chalets, and in a more abstract way, a European perspective on Japanese pavilions. These references combine in such a way that the building is a simple expression of frame, covering and skins.

The dominant element of the design is the projecting structure of the roof that provides protection from the precipitation that annually invades the region, giving the sensation of retreat from the elements.

A marked hierarchy of architectonic elements (covering, structure and glass faces) was fundamental in the interpretation of the closed, pre—existing structure as a development found on the site, a simple, permanent object. Perforated screens emphasize the transparent effect and keep the building as open as possible, while framing views and suggesting intimacy and protection.

The structure's materials were selected to juxtapose stable elements, like glass and stainless steel, with materials more susceptible to substantial modifications or important erosions like the floorboards of the cover, the cedar strips and decks, and the Iroko structure.

In contrast to the intense colors and reflections derived from the site (the green of the fields, the silver-blue of the river, and the dramatic grays and blues of the sky), the building's silver tone changes permanently every time the structure and covering get wet. Later, the sun bleaches it.

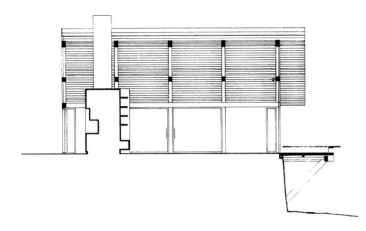

Longitudinal section.

Transverse section.

This house, which has the appearance of a primitive shelter, could be seen as a restrained, yet elegant modern-day interpretation of the very first dwelling.

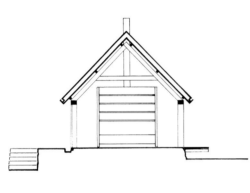

The minimal floor space means that the interior has no need of dividing sections or supporting structures, which would partially block the views of the surrounding countryside.

This is a location which evokes isolation and introspection.

Interaction with the forces of nature is direct and absolute.

There is an immaculate correctness in the way
that the construction has been designed and
carried out; simplicity is the priority here, and
the interplay between the language of the
materials creates a rich, complex world.

The juxtaposition of more stable materials
(for example, stainless steel) with mutable
ones (for example, the wooden dais) is an
important design feature in this structure.

The construction consists of an extension to the summer residence of the Rothschild family. This takes the form of an exterior dining area, a swimming pool and a relaxation space.

## House in Corfu

This summer loggia and swimming pool, commissioned by Lord Jacob Rothschild, was designed as a rest-and-relaxation annex to an already existing house. The structure, located on a promontory on Corfu looking out towards the coast of Albania, offers a stunning view of the sea. From the outset, a priority of the project was to conserve the natural features of the site. This is understandable, given the dramatic nature of the location: a quarry of Venetian marble, with sheer sides. The latter were incorporated into the design of the swimming pool and act as natural watercourses that carry away the pool's overflowing water. As for the overall design, the loggia is strongly influenced by the style of villas which the Romans were accustomed to building in similar locations. Inside, there is a heated swimming pool, while the white open-ended pergola gives shade and shelter to the dining/relaxing area, and includes a kitchen, dressing rooms and bathrooms in the rear. The front part, which opens onto the sea view, is decorated with classical statues, friezes and even a Byzantine mosaic. There is also a series of terraced areas divided up by stone walls, an ancient fountain, and on one side, a stylized entranceway built to look like an ancient ruin. Olive and cypress trees complete the idyllic scene.

The structure contains a number of striking architectural features: strong horizontal lines, the lack of any definite central piece dominating the arrangement, and a structure which makes use of its setting, revealing and framing the natural space and its unique features.

The building stands on a spectacular promontory in Corfu (Greece), not far from the coast of Albania.

The house and the water are inextricably linked.

# Los Vilos

Chile

Christián Boza

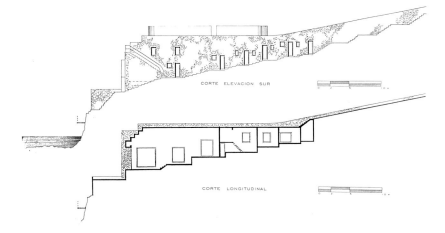

CORTE ELEVACION SUR

CORTE LONGITUDINAL

## House in Los Vilos

Surroundings and topography always have an effect on architecture, but in some cases the relationship between the two is so strong that it is difficult to decide whether we are describing a building or a landscape. This is the case of the house at the top of a cliff near Los Vilos designed by the Chilean architect Cristián Boza. The house is so completely integrated into the surrounding terrain that it is difficult to imagine the landscape without it.

The house has an exceptional site among the rocks, facing the sea and a small island. In this area the coast comes to an abrupt stop, full of steep, jagged edges. Small fjords, coves, craggy rocks and islets dot the seascape, forming a rich and varied visual experience. The small island protects the zone from the open sea, creating a small area of calm waters, perfect for fishing, diving, or collecting shellfish.

Boza first built a path that descends from the highest part of the property, winding its way between the rocks to the edge of the cliff in a series of terraces and graded platforms. The various rooms of the house line this narrow path. The rooms line one side of the path with the cliff on the other side. The series of doors and windows on the curved wall of this exterior corridor give the impression of a narrow village street rather than a single house. At one end of the house at the edge of the cliff, a large volume, houses the living room and dining room, as well as the master bedroom, which is located in the attic. The bedroom can be isolated from the rest of the house by means of a system of sliding wooden doors.

The roof of the house is flat and serves as an enormous terrace which is accessible from both the higher areas of the estate and the path. As Boza himself says: "this terrace is an ideal area for social life". The architect has in fact designed the house on two levels: one interior, with the rooms and another exterior, made up of the terrace, a sculptural yellow wall and the swimming pool. Access to the swimming pool is gained by crossing the wall and walking over a small metal bridge.

At one extreme of the house, at the far end of the cliff, stands an imposing eight-feet-high structure which contains a living room, a dining room and, up in the attic, the main bedroom, which may be either opened or closed by means of a system of sliding wooden doors.

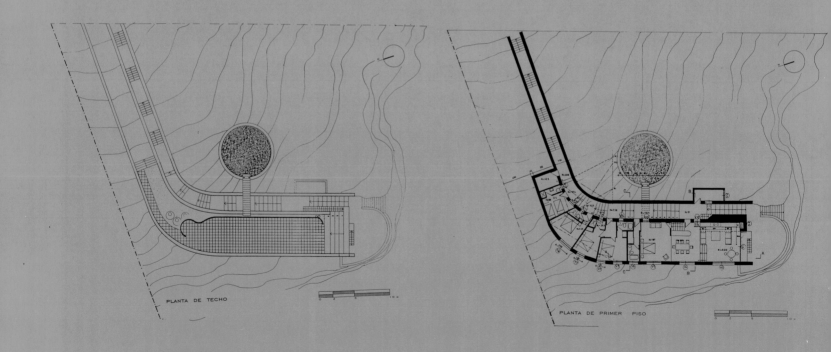

PLANTA DE TECHO

PLANTA DE PRIMER PISO

Note the different levels, the connecting routes between the interior spaces, the beautifully-framed views: this was not an attempt to create a new space, quite the contrary, it came from a process that involved carefully placing a structure within an existing landscape, and making some slight changes to the coast (so that it would be a comfortable place in which to sleep and eat, as well as to sit and wait for sundown in the shade of a wall, gazing out at the ocean). Boza's design tells us nothing new: what it does do is to explore the ability of architecture to bring man closer to nature.

**Sweden** Sandell Sandberg

# Dalarö

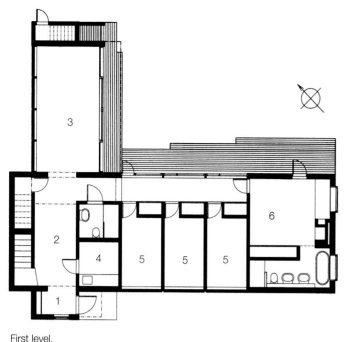

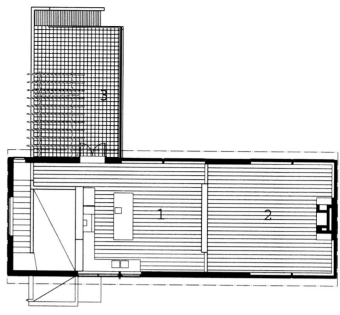

First level.

Second level.

1. Entrance
2. Hall
3. Studio
4. Laundry
5. Bedroom
6. Bedroom

The gallery that runs in front of the bedrooms is a common space that unites the rooms and a transition point between the interior and exterior.

### The Villa at Dalarö

This house is located on a housing estate in Dalarö, to the southeast of Stockholm. The Smadalarövägen road on one side and the sea on the other represent the spatial limits for the house and the garden. The other two sides are bordered by less definite barriers: a tall hedge that follows the path down to the sea, and an open area that looks out to the neighboring houses.

The basic structure is a long, narrow two-story building with a single-story wing attached at a right angle that breaks an otherwise monotonous rhythm. This one-story wing, with its roof terrace, acts as a kind of screen, closing off the garden from traffic and passers-by. The main entrance, which faces south, protrudes slightly from the structure's main block.

Downstairs, the two-story section contains the bedrooms, including three smaller rooms and one master bedroom with an en-suite bathroom and its own fireplace. Each bedroom has access to the garden by way of the gallery.

The second floor is basically an enormous open space crowned by a gabled roof. A large step and a small vertical barrier break up the dining room, where there is a fireplace at one end. As for materials, the foundations of the building have been complicated by soil conditions, and the result is a combination of slabs and poles. Oak appears in the house's interior and exterior. All the doors and windows ar made of oiled oak, and the house's stud-framed structure is covered with horizontal paneling, including some oak sections. Upstairs, the floor is made of stained white oak, while the downstairs floor is concrete. Outside, there is a raised dais of spruce wood in front of the gallery and a hardened surface that serves as a parking space.

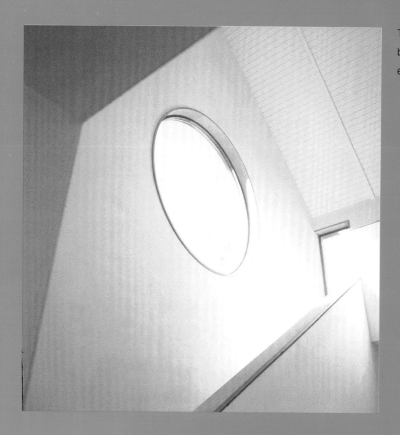

The entrance hall and the staircase are both illuminated by the light that enters through a large circular window.

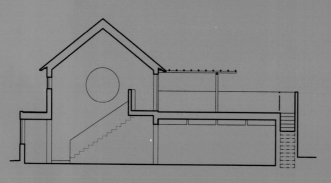

Section showing the access routes of the house.

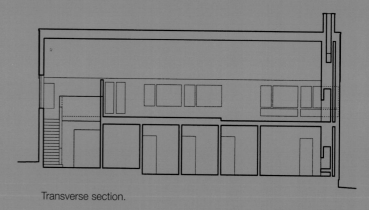

Transverse section.

In the same way that there is a contrast between the two parts of the building, (the large, double-height section with a sloping roof in front of the single-story annex with a flat roof), inside the house the high, open space of the dining-living room on the second story contrasts with the low, fragmented space of the first-story bedroom section.

A v o c a

Grose & Bradley

Australia

69

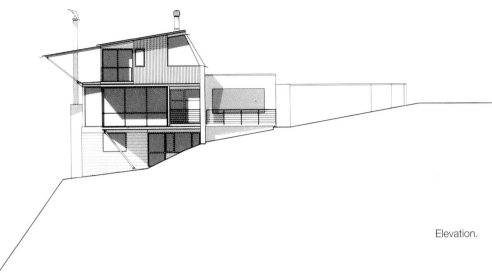

Elevation.

The house is illuminated by a series of windows which allow the sunshine directly into the house. At the same time, the eaves are extended outwards, to provide a certain amount of shade.

## Scobie House

Avoca is a small beachside community north of Sydney, characterized by a ridge that runs parallel to the coastal strip. Scobie House is located at the far end of the ridge, beside a nature reserve, and has a panoramic view of the coast and the Pacific Ocean stretching eastwards. The house is divided into three layers (a similar arrangement to the A3 house in Sydney): the lower level contains the rooms for the children, grandparents and visitors, the hallway and the living room are on the middle level, and the family's bedrooms and studies are on the third level. One important design feature is a wall, aligned north-south, which separates the public space from the private. This wall also contains the house's point of entry, a purposeful device that reveals the view to the visitor only after he or she has arrived.

Inside, the wall gives order to the building. The bathrooms on the middle level are hidden behind it, and it defines the entrance and passageways that connect the living spaces. Structurally, the wall is the large, solid mass that anchors the lighter construction of the upper levels, and helps keep the roof and large awning in place when the strong coastal winds blow.

The deck to the north of the main living room gives the interior spaces the air of a gallery or terrace. The windows on the east wall help define the living room's mood, influenced by the constant changes of light that occur over the course of the day. Towards the west side, the translucent glazing of the louvred gallery ensures the wall's privacy. At the extreme edges of the house, the structure seems to emerge from the surrounding vegetation.

Scobie House hovers on the edge of the ridge and proclaims its integration with the dynamic natural setting, its roof merging with the fragile canopy of eucalyptus trees.

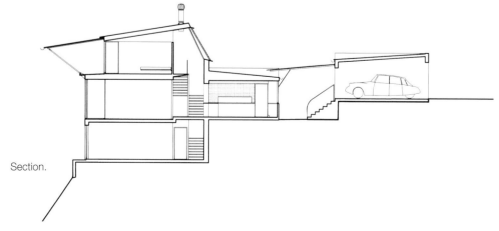

Section.

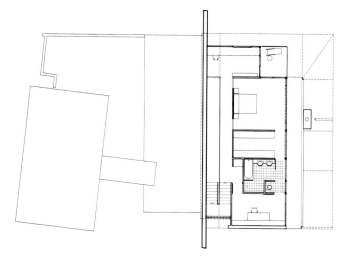

Upper level.

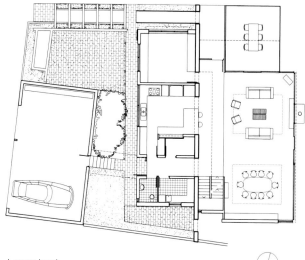

Lower level.

A number of different materials were used in the making of this building in order to come to terms with the gradient of the site: brick for the supporting structures, tubular metal sections for some of the pillars, a metal framework for the roof and eaves, and wood for some of the floor surfaces and interiors.

G r a n a d a

Javier Terrados **77**

## González House

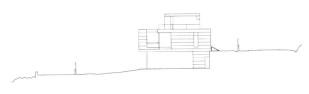

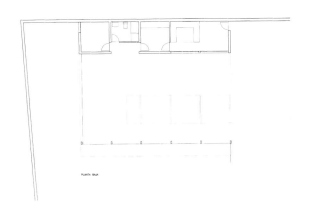

PLANTA BAJA

The entrance provides direct access to the hallway, the kitchen and the bedrooms, which represent the second section.

The lot on which this house stands is located near the sea in Los Yesos, a village south of Granada. It is treated as a diaphanous summer house, open to the exterior so that its inhabitants can be outside as often as possible. The clients wanted to evoke and sustain the memory of what had been their summer activity for many years: traveling by trailer.

This idea became the image that directed and molded the project during its design and execution. To take advantage of the slope, they planned an elongated volume perpendicular to the slope, which is closed towards the mountain and open towards the sea. The volume leans on the upper level of the lot and is elevated on the lower part. As a result, the entire lower floor is a porch, an open space protected from excessive exposure to the sun. They wanted to give the idea of lightness, and thus opted for a well-lit metallic structure between very slender pillars that seem to disappear in the shadow of the porch.

On the upper floor, two rooms with their respective bathrooms share a terrace with magnificent views. The living-dining room and a spacious, semi-covered second terrace are located directly in front of the sea, where the spaces are much more permeable to the exterior.

All the façade's closures that face the sea were resolved in a modular form with aluminum structures that support the sliding glass windows, the blinds and the living room walls.

From the main entrance to the house, on the mountainside, one sees only the two upper levels, which are subtly separated from the floor. A thin line of sea seems to underline the volumes and suggest lightness, movement and air.

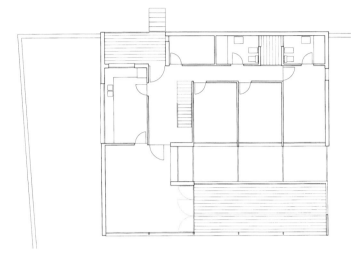

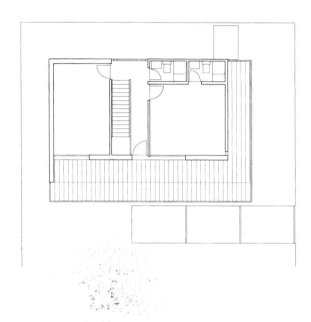

The rooms have been arranged with both the views and the proximity of the house to the sea in mind. On the side facing the mountain, where the living spaces are more closed, there is an elongated section containing the bathrooms and lumber rooms. There is also a point of access at one of the ends of the house.

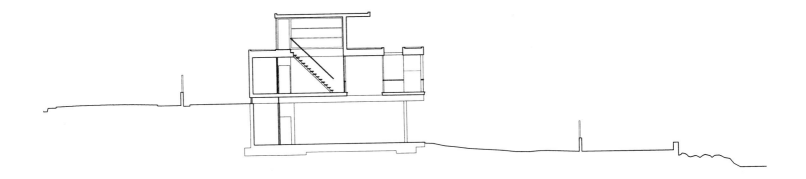

The distinctly horizontal nature of the structure, which is further accentuated by the handrails of the second storey terrace, and the enormous beams that appear to float in the air, all serve to create a sense of movement, as if the house were a caravan, rolling along the coast.

The structure includes a succession of platforms facing onto the sea which give shelter to the exposed areas, while at the same time providing marvellous views. The windows have been arranged differently on each of them, allowing light to flow in and creating a definite spatial connection between the different levels of the dwelling. The design of the terrace that is in front of the living room, on the access storey, has been conceived in such a way that it gives privacy to the rooms without blocking out any part of the beautiful view.

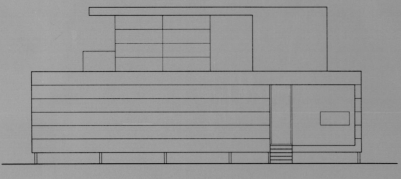

Elevation: main point of access.

Elevation: from the sea.

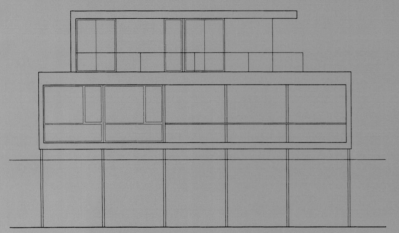

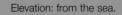

Looking from the main entrance of the house, on the side facing the mountain, only the two upper levels can be seen, and these are subtly separated from the ground: a thin strip of ocean is visible, which effectively underlines the structure; all is lightness, movement and air.

# Tokyo

Japan

Legorreta Arquitectos

## House in Japan

This project is located on a piece of land on the coast south of Tokyo. A Japanese music professor uses it as a second residence and a place to rest. The spaces were designed with this purpose in mind, and give priority to an atmosphere of meditation and tranquility, establishing direct contact with the sea. The architecture's appearance is simple in order to emphasize the marvelous views.

The entrance to the residence is intentionally hidden and has a certain mysterious presence, a common feature in Japanese and Mexican culture. Beyond the entrance is an access tower that leads to a vaulted corridor painted blue. From here, one can descend to the principal space, where the living and dining rooms are located, or one can access the dressing rooms. This central space is characterized by a large opening towards the sea.

The treatment of stone and water and an isolated patio with small dimensions suggest unexpected cultural coincidences. The interior stone-based flooring, the bathrooms, the wood and other special elements were produced in Mexico and exported to Japan. The point was to give each one of the rooms a special character. Cultural interaction played an important role in the design process and construction of the house.

There was also special interest in the relation between the interior and exterior. The terraces became an integral part of both the interior and the landscape. A reservoir surrounds the house and, as a result, water is always present in the design. The exterior is made up of pure white planes with a succession of pinched and ordered volumes along the slope of the ground.

The building looks out westwards across the bay, towards the Pacific ocean, and the main view is of the horizon, where the sky meets the infinite sea. An imposing range of mountains rings the bay and there is a group of houses scattered among some rocky hillocks. This house, situated on top of a small artificial promontory, is cut off from its nearest neighbors to the south by a small road that descends suddenly down towards the sea.

The use of color to emphasize perspective, and the inclusion of brimming sheets of water and channels are features reminiscent of Barragán, who in turn referred back to the ancient tradition of Arabic gardens. The architectural language used here is also reinforced by a series of fleeting quotations and references which lend a richness to the design.

Chile

# C a n t a g u a

Mathias Klotz **93**

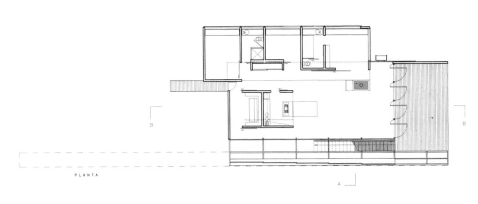
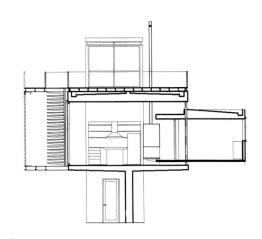

PLANTA

## Reutter House

The Reutter house is situated on a gently sloping wooded site, close to Cachagua beach, 80 miles. from Santiago, Chile.

The building is made up of two horizontal, stained volumes that float and are crossed by a third vertical stone body that acts as a support. In this way, the house is rooted in the ground and rises up among the pines to obtain a privileged view of the Pacific Ocean. The trees protect it from the sun and give more privacy to the terraces and zones with windows.

The two bodies have distinct sizes and materials. The larger volume is made of wood, while the other is covered in corrugated copper. Like a "house within a house," the larger volume contains part of the metallic body. Together, they give the effect of being horizontal and light. A 90 feet bridge that connects the entry-way with the roof, which is also a terrace, further accentuates this effect. A stair-way leads from the covered terrace to the front of the living room on the main floor. The only room on the upper level is a studio situated in a cement structure that hangs cleanly over the terrace.

The living room, dining room and part of the kitchen are united. Only the chimney and a lightweight bookshelf separate the bedroom area, which is contained in a copper volume. The façades that look out to sea and that face the bedrooms are

The priority in the design of this beach house was to reach a balance, a rapport with the natural environment. All of the features of the site have been expoited to the full: the slope, the views and the trees. The materials that have been used for the exterior surfaces were specially chosen to create a harmony between the building and the location.

made entirely of glass, and establish new links between the interior and exterior.

The two boxes are a perfect combination: one houses the private area of the residence — more closed and compact — while the other, transparent and luminous, contains the spaces of family interaction and opens onto the pine woods. There is a second entry where the two buildings meet, without touching, as if they had become dislocated and left a fissure. From there, one can gain easy access to the vestibule that connects all the areas on the first floor.

The piece of concrete is the house's foundation that anchors it to the ground and functions inside the house. In the main floor, it contains the kitchen and separates another room for the TV. On the floor above, it houses a studio with one of its sides completely open to the sea.

A couple of metres away from the north wall (which is the one that receives the most sunshine), there is a wooden framework which serves as a semi-transparent screen that gives privacy to the living room and dining room, while softly filtering the rays of the sun.

Some features, such as the large, wooden roof terrace and thebridge leading down from it to the ground, are clearly based on nautical themes, derived from the coastal location. This construction is dominated by spatial volumes and pure forms, clean lines and natural materials. The interplay between the structure and the elements of the site has the effect of incorporating the house into the landscape.

Kengo Kuma

Japan

# Atami

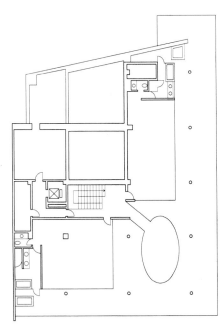

## Water Glass House

The main purpose of the Water Glass House is for guest accommodation. It has three floors, and occupies half of the area of a 120 square feet plot. It is situated on the Atami coast on the edge of a cliff, facing the Pacific Ocean.

Although in the past years, the use of concrete as a construction element is frequent in Japanese architecture, for Kuma it is too heavy and has produced an architecture of monumental form. He has set up the principle of transparency against the use of this material. The materials used are always light, such as glass, steel or wood; they are, according to Kuma, materials of the present.

The floor of the lowest level is covered by a layer of water 35" deep. Three bodies of glass, two square and one oval, have been placed over it and are reflected in the water. They are covered by a metal slat roof. For Kuma, this house does not really have a roof. Nor does it have walls, only some for security reasons. Wherever possible, he has used glass as the construction material. The walls have lost density and have been converted into filters. The intention, on this last floor, was that people should have the sensation of floating on water.

On the lower floor is a Japanese-style room, a room used for administration, a meeting room and a gymnasium. On the access level floor is the dining room, orientated to the south. On the right is the kitchen and the sushi bar, and on the left are the guest rooms. On the last floor, in the two rectangular volumes are the guest rooms and the dining room is in the oval volume.

The origin of the house is a criticism of pre-defined forms, converted into topics of what a villa should be, above all, it forms a reflection of the act of seeing and being seen. The central theme of the Water Glass House is the study of the different ways of seeing, in this case, nature. There is a series of filters and frames which are placed between this and the subject, through which one can see. So, in this way, the materials demonstrate their transparency. There is no watchful object, instead, there are translucent layers which duplicate the images and build up the intermediate space between nature and same subject. The architecture of Kengo Kuma is an experiment into the possibilities of attaining the interior of the very act of seeing. This act of seeing is not watchfulness nor control, but a superposition between the subject and the exterior space. The house is not defines as an object, but as a diversity of spaces resulting from the superposition of different transparencies, crossed by the landscape. Elements, such as the sheet of water which, on the upper level of the house, is mistaken for the sea, far away, or the metal-slatted roof, which tones down the light, are treated as filters or abstract frames and not as obstacles. All this is under the general impression of calm and balance, and an objective use of the materials.

Access to the House of Water and Glass leads from the parking area, through a door gouged out of a granite wall, straight onto a concrete-and-steel bridge. This bridge traverses the space above the sheet of water on the storey below. The rooms of the house are arranged around this vertical, open reception area, where the stairway is located.

The everyday life that goes on inside buildings is, for Kuma, more important than architectural form. Bearing this in mind, the layout of corridors and routes through the house had to arouse as much interest as possible. On the other hand, in this building, nature and the landscape are allowed to share in daily life; in fact, nature takes on a different meaning when it comes into contact with architecture, which gives it a framework. The architecture, therefore, relates openly with the exterior; no clear differentiation is made between what is inside and what is outside. These are not introverted spaces, on the contrary, they interact with the exterior. The architecture is understood, therefore, to be a succession of translucent layers which give the effect of transparency, continuity, and even shade at some points.

On the storey below there is one room laid out in typical Japanese style, another room for administration purposes, a meeting room and a gymnasium. On the storey which is on the same level as the point of access, right in front of the hallway and facing south, is the dining room. On the right are the kitchen and the sushi-bar, and on the left there are the guest rooms. The top storey contains more guest rooms, arranged within two rectangular spaces, while in the oval room there is another dining area.

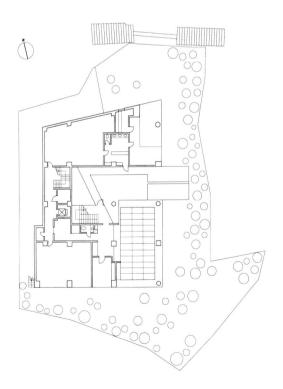

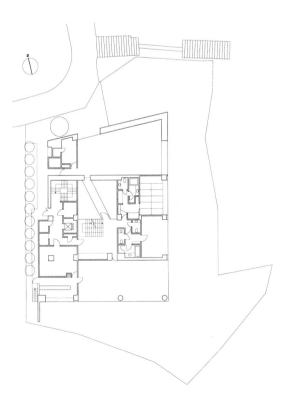

# Capistrano Beach

Rob Wellington Quigley

United States

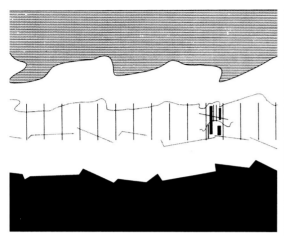

## Capistrano Beach House

Circulation through the house is also full of contrasts in both the interior and exterior. Entrance on the east side is through two iron gates which lead to an intimate, formal vegetable garden enclosed by 6 feet-high glass walls. A concrete "pier" crosses the sand to the porch and front door which face the cliffs and look on to the courtyard garden, perhaps the only "suburban" element in the whole design. The hall follows the curved glass wall and opens dramatically into the spacious living room, with its exposed roof beams and expansive view of the ocean. Along the beach side of the house is a small sitting room shaded by lattice work and a low-ceilinged dining room, both providing more private areas from the living room which through its mahogany and glass doors is almost part of the beach.

In his bid to design authentically Californian architecture, the choice of materials has always been a key issue for Quigley. The stucco and concrete vernacular of early 20th Century Californian architects, like his mentor Irving Gill, has become his trademark. Here, the two-story structure consists of a poured-in-place concrete spine with cantilevered concrete floor slabs. A traditional wood frame clad in black asphalt shingles is used for the bedroom wing. Two guest bedroom suites above the garage are fronted by an asphalt shingle screen. The exposed concrete provides attractive sculptural and geometric shapes both inside and outside: a majestic setting for the fireplace, different levels and walkways in the sand, the striking deco-like concrete spine and so on. As a counter balance to the expanses of concrete and glass, a series of redwood lattice structures, stained grey, are used for cladding or for shade and privacy. Reminiscent of original beach huts, they are just one of the many elements that make this elegant beach house a truly Californian building.

This 3,700 square-foot house has all the apparent glamour of the Californian Dream: large expanses of glass looking over the Pacific Ocean, wooden decks jutting into the dazzling white sand, shady upper decks to enjoy the sea breezes in privacy, a virgin beach for early morning exercise. But under the sound guidance of Rob Quigley, with the "remarkable energy and ethicality that make him the signal architect he is today", there is no chance of it falling into such a clichéd category.

The elongated plot is on a narrow strip of land, merging with the sand to the west, and with a backdrop of high, windswept cliffs to the east. This context is mirrored in the design and in the materials used: the east/west-oriented architectural planes reinforce the rigid, parallel property lines while the north/south elements are more evocative of the surrounding natural forces, the effect of the sea and the wind on the shore and cliffs echoed in gentle curves and eroded, sculptural shapes.

Quigley's designs have always been true to the reality they are in contextually, culturally and climatically. The dramatic and exciting contrasts between the ocean and the land are interpreted architecturally: thick walls of poured concrete set off glass pavilions; deep shade and dappled light as against the dazzling glare of the sand; exposed, extrovert decks and terraces as opposed to quiet, private areas.

# Orta <sub>Italy</sub>

Orta Italy

Mauro Galantino 115

## House in Orta Lake

This project entailed the subtle, delicate restoration of an old building on the edge of Orta Lake, in Italy. The intervention began when Soprintendenza (the official organization in charge of conserving cultural patrimony) granted permission for the renovations, provided they respect volume, coverings and original materials.

Architecturally speaking, there were two goals: first, to bestow residential uses on structures created for other purposes, and secondly, to reconstruct with sensitivity certain architectural features, showing respect for the actual materials but without dismissing the possibility of a radically new perception of the structure. The result is a long, narrow double height living space that stretches out to finish in a covered dock area. The tower, meanwhile, was redesigned as a section containing the bedrooms.

It is worth mentioning that before the renovation began, several elements were still virtually intact, including the original residential section (the end pointing away from the lake), one of the boundary walls, and part of the dock. However, the grade of conservation was terrible. Most of the ironwork had turned to rust, the roof was mostly destroyed and the floor of the first level had tilted and was drifting slowly into the lake. Various investigations concluded that these parts of the building may date back to the 14th Century, except for the dock, which was added in the 19th Century.

Rebuilding the original structure turned out to be much easier. There are hardly any examples left of this type of building: a residential–productive microcosm in which the bedrooms, kitchen and living space were all arranged vertically in the tower, with the stable below. A henhouse, garden, dry dock for the boat, and the landing stage were located towards the lake.

The plans illustrate the unusual elongated geometry of the building, as well as the sum effect produced by the different parts.

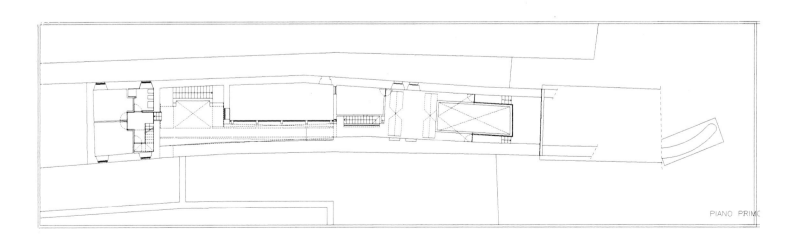

PIANO PRIMO

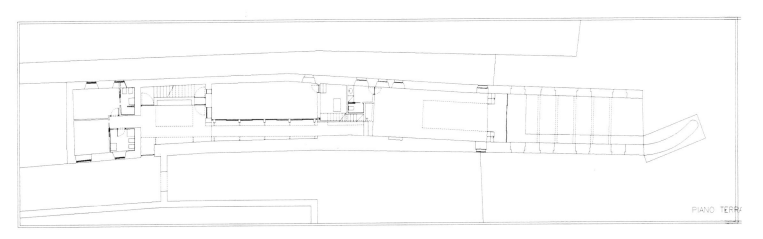

PIANO TERRA

The addition of high catwalk-corridors, as well as the quality of the materials and the workmanship have gone a long way to making this project a simple but very effective exercise in renovation. The ultra-modern metal catwalks cut the high, white walled space into two levels, with the exposed beams of the gable roof above providing a stylistic contrast.

The renovation's overall effect is new spaces defined through clear, concise geometry that contrast with the pre-existing structure. Following the longitudinal axis, the building is a succession of well-connected volumes that harmonize yet maintain their independent existence. The plan is truly the sum of its spaces, each defined by a specific peculiarity. For example, the double-height ceiling in the living space is punctuated partway up by the exposed catwalks, while the dock is a unique space that is neither interior nor exterior. Meanwhile, the roof, resting on wooden beams and held by steel tensors, floats above the succession of volumes below and manages to appear simultaneously continuous and independent.

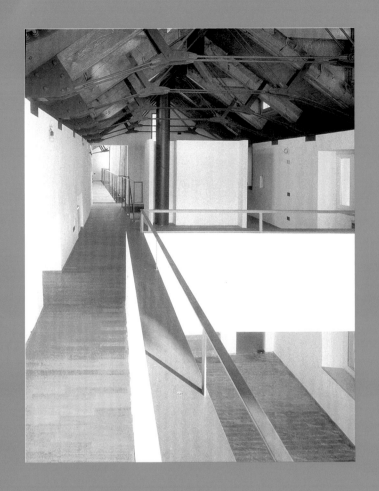

SEZIONE LONGITUDINALE

Portugal

# Quinta da Moura-Caxias

Aires Mateus

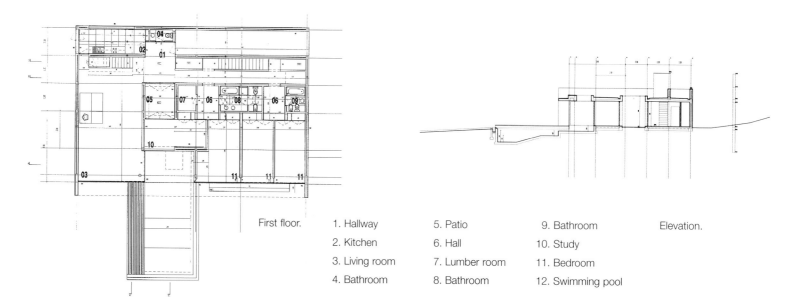

First floor.

| 1. Hallway | 5. Patio | 9. Bathroom | Elevation. |
| 2. Kitchen | 6. Hall | 10. Study | |
| 3. Living room | 7. Lumber room | 11. Bedroom | |
| 4. Bathroom | 8. Bathroom | 12. Swimming pool | |

## Quinta da Moura House

The basic layout of this house is conventional. The site is virtually square, with a compulsory building zone in the center. While the house is accessed from the north, the structure is mostly closed on the north side and open to the south, where there are marvelous views. The south side enjoys abundant sunshine and an unhindered view of open space and the sea. Two high dihedral walls enclose the structure and almost completely shut off three sides. The arrangement of these two walls forms the entrance: white walls flank a wooden surface, which holds the door.

The entrance section contains the guest bathroom and the kitchen. The routes that connect the interior spaces run parallel to the entry. A passageway, which rises from the garage on the lower story up to the sun-drenched terrace, represents house's largest dimension. The parallel corridor runs along the level and links the living room to the bedrooms.

The second important section evokes the connection between the house and the water nearby. Coming through the front door, the observer sees the patio, with the study beyond it. Beyond the study is a swimming pool, and beyond that, the sea. This perspective gives the house depth and links the liquid to the solid. On the south side, all the interior spaces fan out towards the sea view. The living spaces are arranged according to basic structural principles: they are peaceful, unassuming areas that emphasize the corridors as lines of motion. The resulting spatial logic goes beyond the house's physical layout.

Almost all the sections and details of this very simple construction are painted white, resulting in a display of ever-changing shadows that drift across the planes. The only non-white element is the floor surface: long, pale wooden strips for most of the house, which become stone tiles as the water draws near.

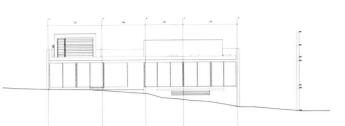

Longitudinal section. This diagram shows the progression of spaces down towards the swimming pool and the sea. This succession of different living spaces draws the observer's gaze out into the surrounding countryside.

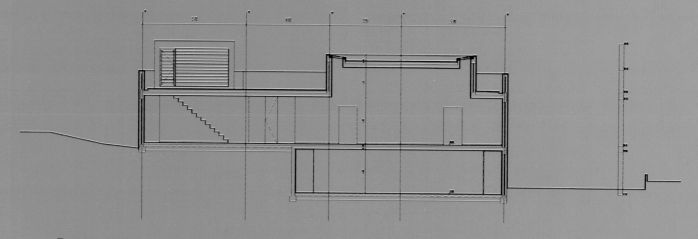

Transverse section.

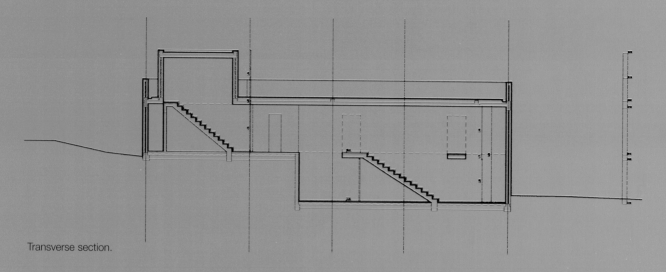

Transverse section.

The north and south walls are counterposed both functionally and formally. The north face contains the entrance to the house, which is opaque. The south face, however, is open and transparent, and offers some magnificent views of the sea.

# Calella de Palafrugell

**Spain**

Josep Maria Bosch Reig, Lluís Jubert and Eugènia Santacana

127

First floor of the
construction and
exterior views.

## House at Calella de Palafrugell

The architect Josep Maria Bosch Reig built this house in 1965 as a weekend retreat for two families. Situated by the Mediterranean, just outside the town of Calella de Palafrugell on the Costa Brava, the house sits on a piece of land with a steep slope. The architect responded to the terrain by creating terraces at different levels, all with excellent views.

The original layout consisted of two houses. The first was a ground-floor residence with a small apartment above for guests. The apartment had an independent access, and an interior stairway joined the two levels. The other house had the opposite layout: the main residence on the second story and a small guest apartment downstairs. The renovation program carried out by the architects Lluis Jubert and Eugènia Santacana is an attempt to maintain the original style of the house and to modify the layout only where necessary, adapting it to the new needs of the two families. In both houses, the guest apartment was redesigned as an area containing bedrooms and bathrooms, so that all of the living spaces would have access to the gardens and enjoy views of the sea.

The garden areas were enlarged and made to face the sea. Each of the living spaces has a subtly different view of the exterior. The main materials used in the renovation process were: Jatova wood for the interior floor surface, Iroko wood for the exterior deck, a white aluminum shutter system to regulate the amount of sunshine coming through, white plaster walls, and new glass, transparent handrails which do not obstruct the sea views.

Partial views of the house
from one of the boundaries of
this large, sheer-sided site.

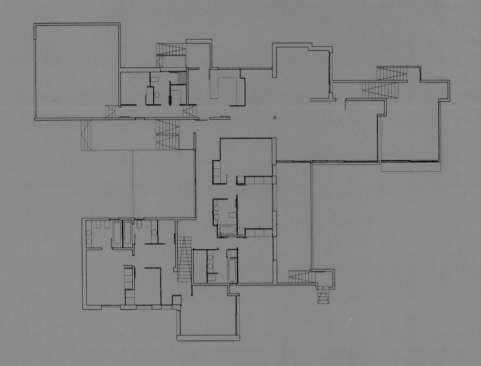

Plan of the first level.
Views of the living room
and bathroom.

This extremely comprehensive plan specifies a careful process for the interior renovation of an existing structure, to make the interior more habitable (quality of materials, organization and fluidity of spaces) as well as adding certain maritime touches.

The bareness of the spaces and the simple, refined design are the outstanding features of this interior renovation project.

Byron Bay

Australia

Grose & Bradley

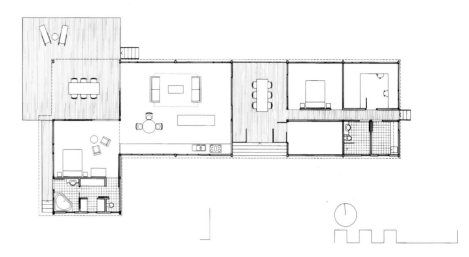

General plan of the house and various exterior views.

## Steel House

The Steel House stands high on a ridge that looks south towards Byron Bay, Australia's most easterly point, and north towards the Gold Coast. The occupants, however, decided to orient the house towards the east, with a view that looks straight into the rising sun. To some degree, this decision determined the building's architecture.

Another aspect that influenced the overall design was their desire to live in the fresh air, in the middle of beautiful countryside. This house is like a primitive platform that rises above the natural world.

The actual form of the house is self-evident, stripped of any complications. It is a minimal structure, in keeping with the Australian rural tradition and the appropriate environmental controls. To create the idea of a house situated in the middle of the wilds of nature, the exterior walls are basically flat with fixed, practical windows and blinds to keep out the early morning light.

The design has its own climatic logic. During the winter, the morning sun spreads warmth throughout the interior of the platform-house. In the summer, the blinds are pulled shut, creating deep shadows that cool the interior and draw attention to the view out the windows on the shaded side of the building, where the blinds are left up.

The building appears to have been recently constructed. The original galvanized steel structure has a rough, untreated look to it, a feature accentuated by the vertical zinc sheets that line the outside walls. These materials and their industrial, unrefined finishes make the building seem like some kind of rigorous man-made object. Yet perhaps this is the only possible architectural response to such an overwhelming landscape.

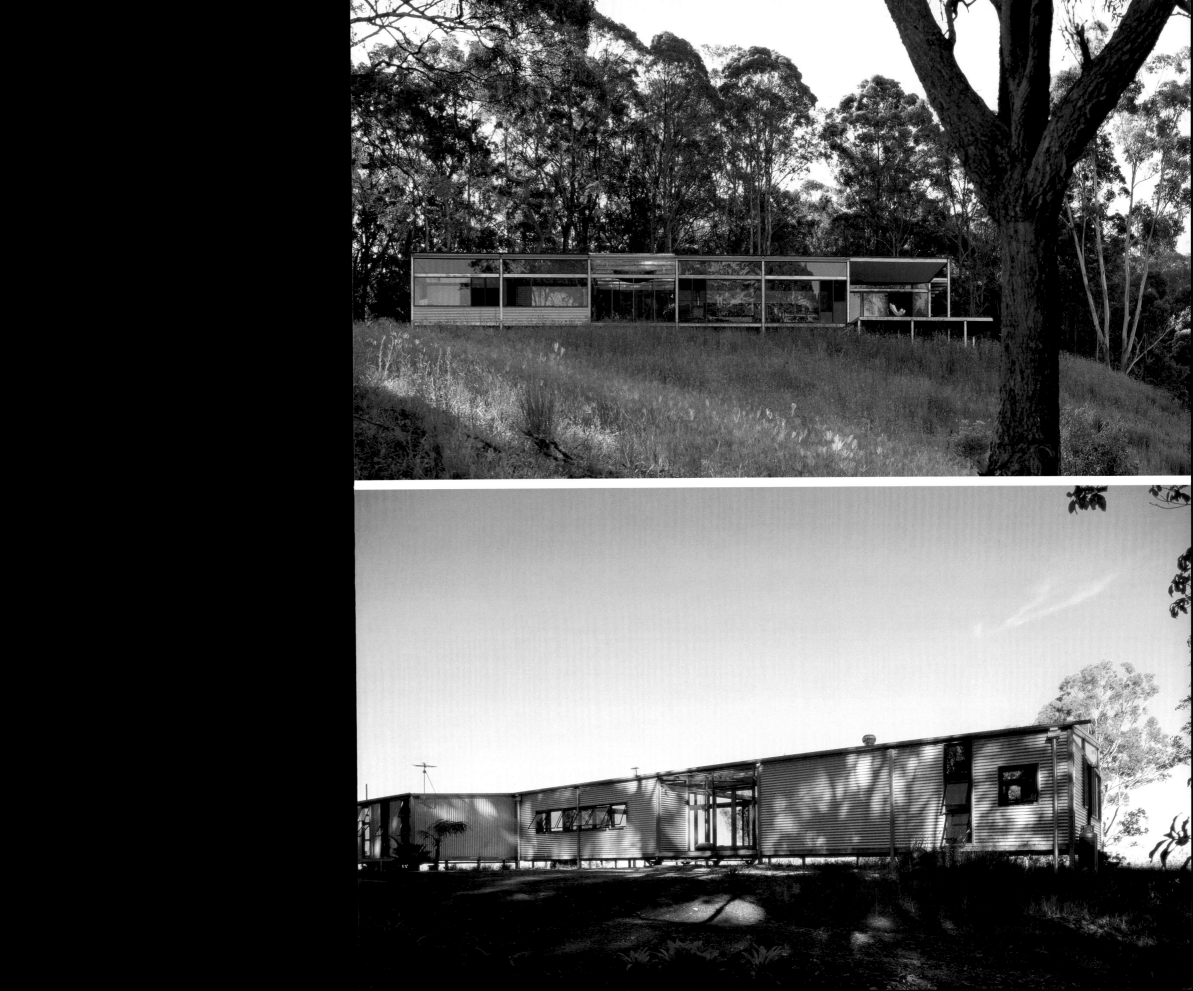

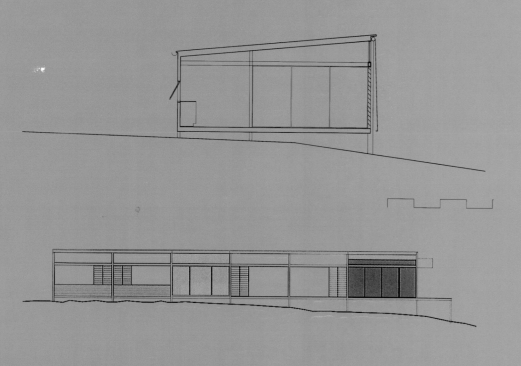

*Right page, top:*
The modulation of the structure and
the inclusion of the metal sheet result in
a clear, concise volumetry.

Transverse section and main elevation.

Several views of the central connecting space,
which was devised as a semi-exterior area.

The house is a simple volumetric space rising from a powerful, fantastic landscape.

# North Devon

Hudson Featherstone

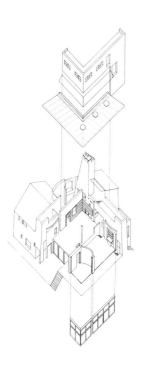

## Baggy House

The most striking feature of this house's location is the contrast between the views. One side contemplates the south and east, where the rolling Devon countryside spills into the distance, while on the north side, the land climbs towards Middleborough Hill. From the very first sketches, the architect played with the idea of a house with two faces: one side more opaque, and the other more transparent, gazing out at the sun, sea and mountains.

The north façade protects an old converted stable, which is now a section of rooms. This represents the "solid" side seen upon arrival that hides the view of the sea, giving privacy to the interior. The opaque effect is achieved by means of low, compact forms, slate tiles, small windows, and an imposing chimney. Through the main door, there is a hallway with a low ceiling dominated by a granite column. The staircase, bathed in natural light, leads up to the second floor and to an arrangement of rooms with south facing views. Glass screens frame the views and can be opened up in summer to convert the living room into an airy summerhouse overlooking the ocean. This is the real heart of the building: all the other rooms and corridors spread out from here. It is also the element that links the opaque side to the transparent section.

The building's form and construction were heavily influenced by the geography of the site. The thick walls on the north side insulate the house from the bitter winter winds, while the walls on the south side, subtly constructed out of steel, wood and glass, enhance the warmth and light of the sun's rays and provide ventilation for the rest of the house.

This house has an exceptional location – high up on a promontory, with a panoramic view of the Atlantic ocean. In the 19th century it was home to the founder of The Birmingham Post, later it became a hotel, but then the present owners decided to convert it back into a private house. It was decided right from the start to reconstruct the building, given that the original structure was architecturally fairly charmless.

The prominent position of the building and the spectacular countryside and seascapes around it were significant factors that influenced the design process. The guidelines for the plans were clear: it was to be a six-bedroom family house with plenty of room for guests, while the design should incorporate as much of the location as possible. Fortunately, the client was open to ideas.

The views differ considerably when seen from the various levels, modified by the horizontal glass rectangles arranged on the southern face of this split-personality construction.

At the lowest, most sheltered point of
the site there is a pond-garden, which
was laid on top of an existing rock
garden. Seen from the main section of
the house, the pink wall that rises
skywards from the far end of the
swimming pool makes an impressive
contrast with the drystone walls nearer
to the building, and this pink barrier
serves to protect the swimming pool
from prying eyes.

The pool, with its linear form,
stretches out towards the lower
section of the garden. Other objects,
such as the terrace or the shower,
were included as sculptural creations
that harmonize with the rolling
landscape. The pond-garden is an
exercise in the juxtaposition of natural
and artificial materials. The paved
area that leads out towards the
hidden garden is made up of
prefabricated concrete sections.

The concrete diving board, the
waterfall and the steps were
constructed in situ, all of them
arranged along the massive pink
expanse emerging from the water.
There are wooden platforms and a
slate bridge arranged within the pool,
which define and separate the space.

Xavier Barba

M

konos

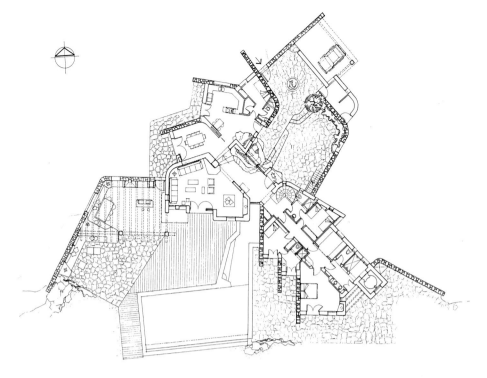

## Tsirigakis House

A family retreat, this house is located on the highlands of Mikonos, away from the hordes of tourists that swarm around the port. This is an earthquake zone, so the house is built out of reinforced concrete. However, this is not the only form of protection that the house needs: the fierce winds that whip in from the Aegean have also affected the design, causing the walls of the house to stretch out like protective arms that shelter the swimming pool and surround the patio. Most of the surfaces are dressed in local rock, a feature that unites the structure with the land and makes it easier to maintain. However, part of the exterior has been finished in the smooth white stucco so typical of the Greek islands. The stucco contrasts sharply with the exposed stonework and is a time-honored method of keeping the house cool.

When seen from a distance, the house almost seems to fade into the dry rock of the island, leaving in sight only a few of the white, sensually rounded walls, the dome above the bathroom and the characteristic chimneys that shoot up from the flat construction. A traditional roof of woven branches shades the terrace looking out onto the port.

The interior, which is 2150 square feet in size, is comprised of a living/dining room, a master bedroom suite and three guest rooms on the main floor, with another two-bedroom apartment below for the son of the family and his guests. The interior is a space illuminated by natural light and enclosed by white walls, arches and columns, with a traditional wooden-beamed roof above and terra cotta floor tiles below. A short flight of steps and a low wall separate the dining room from the living room.

Among the defining elements in the design of the house are the use of whitewashed stucco to envelop the gentle, rounded shapes, and the inclusion of dry, rocky walls as main features of the volumetry and the exterior surfaces.

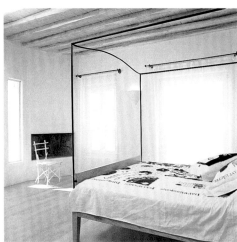

Philippe Meier

# Mies, Léman Lake

Switzerland

It was just a small wooden construction facing Montblanc; a little cabin that grew and grew until it turned into a summer house.

plan
0      2,5

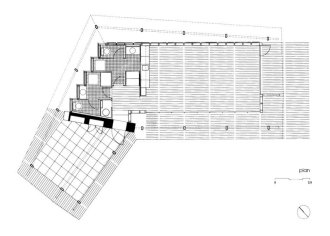

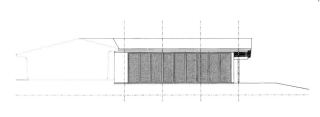

Planta y alzados.

## Summer House

The Swiss architect Georges Addor built the original cabin in the 1950's. What makes the building interesting is the plasticity of the woodwork. Also, by experimenting with the asymmetry of the main beams – one is mounted horizontally while the other tilts towards the floor – the architect made an otherwise uninteresting roof dynamic. Likewise, he included a brick fireplace to break up the interior geometry.

The new extension contains two bathrooms and dressing rooms, plus a large living room and kitchen with views of the lake and the surrounding landscape. The structural alterations are rooted in Addor's original designs, especially the plasticity of the new section. The addition of a new volume perpendicular to the lake gives the house an "L" shape. This feature proved to be one of the project's most important architectural decisions.

The structure is an orthogonal box set below a roof designed along the same lines as the existing one. On the exterior, pine slats painted the favorite nautical color, white, make up the sides beneath the left main beam. White DM wood panels are used on the sides that open onto the surrounding landscape. There is a kind of recessed façade arrangement(which looks like it is made up of scales) that increases the natural light and ventilation for the bathrooms, which are hidden on a slightly lower level out of sight from the house. There are two main types of glass adornments: a huge, fixed glass section with a small, inserted door-window looks out towards the lake, and on the garden side, a glass expanse slides back, concertina-style, to give spatial continuity to the interior and exterior.

A dais of Iroko wood skirts the small building. This material, with definite naval connotations, can also be found inside as part of the flooring. All materials are presented in their natural state: untreated Iroko parquet, vertical sheets of unpolished, sawed red cedar, gray melamine for the doors and kitchen and stainless steel door fittings.

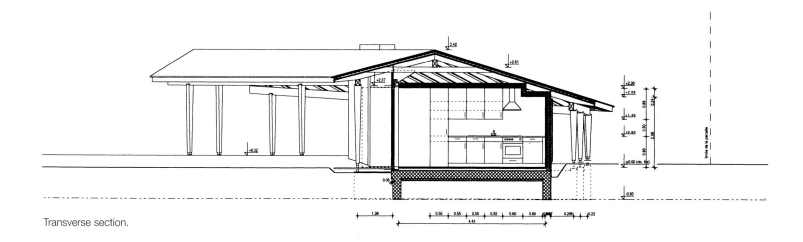

Transverse section.

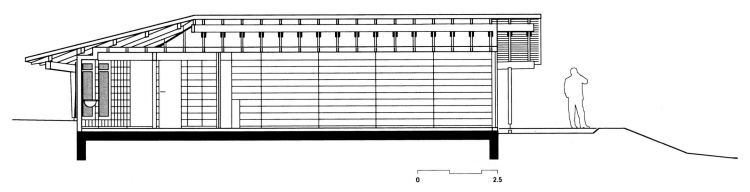

0          2.5

Longitudinal section.

The general use of the wood, the detailed treatment of the enclosures (both the woodwork and the facings of the new pillars) represent part of a new architectural vocabulary, simple in approach, complicated in resolution, and which lends continuity and richness to the existing structure.

The summerhouse's privileged location, right by the lakeside, perfectly justifies the new geometric outline of its arrangement.

This new section, both minimal and subtle, drags the cabin out of the 1950's and turns it into an exquisite living space

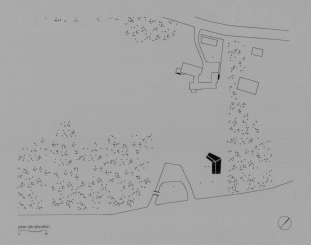

plan de situation

Liesbeth and Juul Norgaard

# Copenhagen Port

**Denmark**

The stairway, which looks like a slash in the ironwork, and the skylight, another cut in the roof, lie parallel to each other and lengthwise along the house.

## Boathouse

An unusual plan with surprising results – the transformation of a living space into a structure resembling a boat moored at the water's edge. The typical characteristics of the seagoing life, change, flux and nomadism, are used here to explore just how much a large vessel can be adapted for a family's residential purposes.

Just as when building on terra firma, the architectural priorities were those of optimum light, adequate ventilation and spaciousness. Another important feature was access to nature, specifically the changing colors of the light on the water and in the sky.

Traditional materials and building techniques seemed appropriate– Douglas pine wood for the walls and floors and Red Godoya and Bangkirai for the terrace and stairway. The boathouse is divided into two levels, with terraces on the lower level, and a total floor space of 2,500 square feet. The spacious hallway on the first floor connects with a study–bedroom and bathroom, while there is a large stairway in the middle of the boat that leads to the living room, kitchen and dining room on the second floor. The boathouse is always flooded with light thanks to the enormous windows, glass doors and especially the rectangular skylight mounted lengthwise on the roof. The ample light produces reflections in the interior that seem to recreate a submarine world. Due to the arrangement of windows, every room has an excellent view, including some views of the 18th Century buildings on the Copenhagen seafront. The exterior landscape is so impressive, in fact, that it almost makes one forget the interior of the boat, with its strictly minimal furnishings. The walls are either made of wood, painted a very transparent white or coated in a pale blue whitewash.

The houseboat is firmly rooted, or anchored, in the Copenhagen port, and forms part of a small community of houses that float alongside each other, sharing the shame rhythm of life, in harmony with their environment.

Unlike its neighbors, this boathouse is permanently beached in this little corner of the Copenhagen port.

Unlike its neighbours in the foreground of the
photograph, the boat-house is permanently beached
in this little corner of the port of Copenhagen.

The fact that almost all of the partition walls are glazed means that there is an abundance of natural light. In addition, thanks to the location of the house, there was no need to hang curtains or net curtains, which would have spoiled the views.

Hans Peter Wörndl

# Mordsee
# Lake

**Autria**

## Gucklhupf

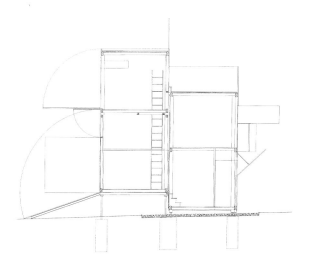

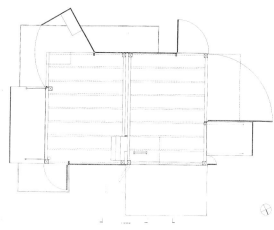

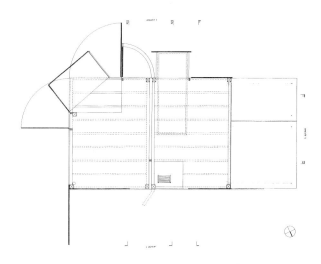

Plans and sections.

"Space is uncertainty. I constantly have to draw its limits, define it. It never belongs to me, is never is given to me. I have to conquer it." Georges Perec

If one of the first things we do with unknown things is to give them a name, then it is necessary to explain the origin of the strange name of this wooden box, a viewpoint in front of the beautiful Mondsee Lake in Austria. Its name refers to two things: a hill close to the site that is called Gucklhupf, and a traditional Austrian pastry, Gucklhupf, that is customarily eaten on Sundays. Both names refer to the action of looking down or observing from a place thought to give a better point of view. The Gucklhupf first came about as an idea to take part in an event in summer 1993 called the Festival of the Regions, in which all kinds of cultural, artistic and architectural works participate. The festival's general theme to develop was "the strange." Wörndl took advantage of a relative's lot beside the Mondsee Lake to construct this fantastic, three–dimensional experiment.

The architect and two collaborators constructed the box using plans that were constantly modified. They resolved details by giving them form. They improvised often and decided upon some details while working and left others pending, to resolve in the future. The idea was to create a living object that would be in constant transformation, even after it was finished, and that would establish a dialogue with the landscape.

The Gucklhupf is a cubical wood structure measuring approximately 13 x 20 x 23 feet, sheathed in plywood and protected with a varnish used on boats. Many of its faces are mobile and can be manipulated by visitors to reveal the surrounding landscape. In the Gucklhupf, the plans vary and constantly modify the space, in the same way that the building relates to its surroundings.

Despite the fact that the local authorities provisionally approved the Wörndl work as a permanent sculptural object and space for exhibitions on the site, the area residents opposed it and pressured authorities to revoke their decision. The Gucklhupf was thus requalified as a "building" and considered illegal according to the demanding regulations. The building was impossible to keep. After numerous discussions and expert debates, the issue ended in an administrative court that did not consider it necessary to fine the architect for the lawsuit brought against him. In spite of this, the patrimony commission rejected his position and ordered him to remove the work.

A neighboring community offered Wörndl an alternative site, but they could not agree on the method that should be used to move it. In the end, as the controversy continued and for reasons of time and money, the structure was dismantled. It is currently stored, to be reconstructed on another landscape where it can begin a new dialogue.

The structure was built by the architect and two assistants, using plans which were constantly undergoing alterations. Smaller details were added as the structure took shape, which involved a great deal of improvisation and spontaneous decision-making. Other details were left unfinished, to be decided in the future. The idea was to create a living object, a construction that would seem to be in constant transformation, even after completion, and which would at the same time harmonise and contrast with the natural surroundings.